BENCHMARK BIOGRAPHIES

A Life with Animals
JANE GOODALL

by Elizabeth Ferber

MARSHALL CAVENDISH
NEW YORK

Benchmark Books
Marshall Cavendish Corporation
99 White Plains Road
Tarrytown, New York 10591-9001

© Marshall Cavendish Corporation 1997

Library of Congress Cataloging-in-Publication Data
Ferber, Elizabeth, date
Jane Goodall : a life with animals / by Elizabeth Ferber.
p.   cm. — (Benchmark biographies)
Includes bibliographical references and index.
Summary: Examines the personal and professional life of the noted zoologist
and describes her work with the chimpanzees of Tanzania.
ISBN 0-7614-0489-9 (lib. bdg.)
1. Goodall, Jane, 1934-   —Juvenile literature. 2. Primatologists—England—Biography—Juvenile literature.
3. Chimpanzees—Tanzania—Gombe Stream National Park—Juvenile literature. [l. Goodall, Jane, 1934-   .
2. Zoologists. 3. Chimpanzees—Habits and behavior. 4. Women—Biography.] I. Title. II. Series.
QL31.G58F47   1997   591'.092—dc20   [B]   96-17131   CIP   AC

Photo research by Sheila Buff

Photo Credits
Front cover: Jane Goodall, courtesy National Geographic Society; back cover: courtesy of ©Gerry Ellis Nature
Photography; pages 6, 18: ©Tim Laman/The Wildlife Collection; pages 9, 25, 31(top): Gerry EllisNature
Photography; pages 15, 34, 36: Archive Photos; pages 22, 23, 28, 33, 35, 38, 43: Jane Goodall, Courtesy
National Geographic Society; pages 26, 30, 31(bottom), 42: © John Giustina/The Wildlife Collection;
page 37: UPI/BETTMANN

Printed in Hong Kong

1   3   5   6   4   2

For Gideon

CONTENTS

A loud clear wail is a chimpanzee's way of saying, "Danger! Stay away!"

BEGINNINGS:
THE LOVE OF ANIMALS

DANGER IN THE FOREST

Jane Goodall walked through the dense, lush forest as the rain beat down. Suddenly she saw a chimpanzee hunched not far in front of her. This young English scientist had been studying communities of chimpanzees in Africa for several years. Now, fearing for her safety, she froze, waiting to see what would happen.

She heard a sound above her, looked up, and saw a second chimp high in a tree overhead. When the chimp in the branches saw her, he gave out a loud clear wail—*wraaaah*—the call that chimpanzees use to scare away other animals.

Out of the corner of her eye to the right, Jane could make out a pair of dark, gleaming eyes staring through the thick brush and a black hand shaking a branch in warning: "Don't come any closer," it seemed to caution. Just then, behind her, came another loud *wraaaah* and above her the chimp in the tree began to sway the rain-heavy branches. She was surrounded on all sides by wary chimps. Slowly, she crouched down and tried to appear as nonthreatening as possible to the animals.

Moments later, the chimp directly ahead charged at her. His hair bristled, clearly showing his anger. Just as the dark, wet animal neared Jane, he swerved to one side and ran off into the forest. The scientist remained quiet and as still as she could as two more chimps charged and then ran off. After a short while, Jane realized, with much relief, that she was alone again. The chimps that had surrounded her had all run off into the dense brush. Slowly and shakily she got up and resumed her trek through the forest in the rain.

THE LIFE OF AN EARLY ANIMAL LOVER

Jane Goodall was born in London, England on April 3, 1934, where she lived for a short while before her parents Mortimer and Myfanwe—called Vanne—moved to a house just outside the city. When Jane was five and her sister, Judy, was one, the Goodall family moved to France. Their parents wanted Jane and Judy to learn French, but their plan to stay in France ended when World War II began.

The Goodalls moved back to England, but their house had been sold. Jane's father, who was an engineer and loved to race cars, moved his family to the old manor house where he had grown up. The grounds had the ruins of an old castle, geese grazing on the big lawn, and a small wooden house full of egg-laying

A pair of chimps take refuge in the dense brush.

hens. In nearby fields, cows and horses munched on grass and Jane would wander for hours watching the animals.

During World War II, Jane's father joined the army to fight for England against Germany. Jane, her mother, and her sister went to live with their other grandmother in another grand manor house called *The Birches* in the city of Bournemouth on the southern coast of England. Jane spent her childhood and teenage years living there, and she loved to go out on the cliffs and down to the beach near the house. She also enjoyed sitting in the garden behind the house, watching the birds in a beech tree and listening to their songs.

Jane's mother had always encouraged her to read books, and one of her favorites was *The Story of Doctor Dolittle* by Hugh Lofting. It is a tale about a veterinarian who learns how to talk with his patients. Part of the book takes place in Africa. Jane decided, after reading the story several times, that one day she would travel to the continent so wonderfully described in *The Story of Doctor Dolittle.*

After reading about Doctor Dolittle, Jane read as many books as she could about animals. She loved tales about wolves, bears, wolverines, orangutans, and elephants to name a few. Another much-loved book was Rudyard Kipling's *The Jungle Book,* which tells the story of Mowgli, a boy who is raised in the jungle by animals. Of course, the Tarzan books by Edgar Rice Burroughs had a special place on her shelf as well.

Jane dreamed of seeing animals, not

just in zoos, but in the wild where they lived. She watched the wild creatures near her home, and even started a nature group, called the Alligator Club. The club went on nature walks, camped out in Jane's garden, and wrote down what they observed animals doing.

While Jane was in school, she worked at a stable in exchange for riding the horses and ponies. She loved being around the animals and worked very hard, cleaning out stalls, shining tack, and feeding the horses.

The most important animal in Jane's early life was a dog named Rusty. Rusty lived in a hotel around the corner from *The Birches* and Jane spent many afternoons teaching Rusty how to shake, roll over, and jump through a hoop. Jane also dressed Rusty in clothes and read stories to him. She has said, "Rusty taught me so much about animal behavior, lessons that I have remembered all my life." Little did Jane know that she would grow up to be one of the world's most famous *ethologists*. An ethologist is a person who studies the way animals live and why they behave the way they do.

TRANSITIONS: FINDING HER WAY

BEYOND SCHOOL

Jane received very good grades in high school, especially in the subjects that interested her the most, history and biology. When she finished school at eighteen, Jane did not know what she wanted to do other than observe and write about animals.

She spent a few months in Germany, living with a German family and learning a little bit of the language. When she returned to England, Jane went to secretarial school in London because her mother had told her that secretaries could get jobs anywhere in the world.

After she got her diploma, Jane worked at a clinic for children with physical disorders. The clinic, which was located in Bournemouth, served the needs of children who had paralyzed limbs from polio, muscular dystrophy, and other muscle disorders. Working in the clinic Jane learned, most importantly, how lucky she was to have a healthy body.

Next, she found a secretarial job at

Oxford University, a school that she wished she could attend, but did not have the money. The river at Oxford was her favorite part of the school. In the mornings or late in the evenings, she would paddle a canoe, watching all the water birds, which included moorhens, kingfishers, and swans.

After she spent a year at Oxford, Jane returned to London and worked at a film studio that made documentary films. Her parents had divorced by this point, and Jane lived in her father's apartment. She learned much about filmmaking while working at the studio, and she enjoyed her job very much, but she had not forgotten her dream to go to Africa. In fact, Jane still read as many books as she could about Africa and the animals that lived there.

GOING TO AFRICA

One Wednesday morning, while Jane was living and working in London, she received a letter from an old school friend named Clo. Clo, who was living in Africa on a farm her parents had bought in Kenya, invited Jane to visit. Jane accepted immediately, but first she had to earn the money to pay for her journey.

Jane moved back to Bournemouth, where she worked as a waitress in an old-fashioned hotel near *The Birches*. After four months of waiting tables, she had enough money saved to pay for a round-trip fare to Africa.

Jane was twenty-three when she first sailed to the continent of Africa on a large ocean liner named the *Kenya Castle*. She loved watching the sea from the deck of the ship, occasionally catching glimpses of dolphins, sharks, and flying fish. The *Kenya Castle* came into port in Mombasa, Kenya, twenty-one days after it had left London and from there Jane took a train to Nairobi, Kenya's capital city.

Clo met Jane at the train in Nairobi, and on their way to the farm, the young animal lover caught her first glimpse of a giraffe up close. "When I saw him," Jane said, "that amazing long, long animal, I finally knew for sure, that I was really there. I had actually gotten to the Africa of my dreams—the Africa of Doctor Dolittle and Tarzan."

AN AFRICAN YEAR

Jane spent a few weeks on Clo's farm, but then returned to Nairobi where she started a temporary job that she had arranged for herself while still in England. The job was boring, but Jane could support herself in Africa while figuring out how to work with animals.

After two months in Kenya, Jane met the man who would start her on her life-long career with animals. A friend of Jane's introduced her to Dr. Louis Leakey, a famous anthropologist (a person who studies the behavior of human beings) and paleontologist (someone who studies fossils), who was working in Kenya. Jane first met Dr. Leakey in his big, messy office which held old bones, teeth, and scattered papers.

Dr. Leakey's secretary had just resigned, so he offered the job to the young, blonde Englishwoman. Dr. Leakey was very impressed by how much

Jane knew about animals and took her to Nairobi National Park, where there were scores of animals to observe.

In 1957, before Jane began working for Dr. Leakey at the museum, he and his wife, Mary, took her on a trip to the famous Olduvai Gorge. There was no road leading into the gorge, so the Leakeys, Jane and another young woman who worked at the museum had to drive straight over the land. The Leakeys had been going to the Olduvai Gorge for many years to look for fossils and usually spent several months digging in the hot sun and dry dirt. While visiting the gorge, Jane saw lions and hyenas and declared, "I had never been so happy. There I was, far from any human dwellings, out in the wilds of Africa, with animals all around me in

World renowned anthropologist and paleontologist, Dr. Louis Leakey, shows off a few of his fossil finds.

the night. Wild, free animals. That was what I had dreamed of all my life."

Once she got back to Nairobi, Jane began her new job. She and a friend from England, Sally, shared an apartment and immediately started collecting animals of their own. At one point, they had a bush baby (a squirrel-like animal closely related to a monkey), a vervet monkey, a dwarf mongoose, a hedgehog, a white and black rat, a cocker spaniel, a springer spaniel, and a Siamese cat.. Jane and Sally often drove to the Langata Forest, near the Leakeys' home, with a car full of animals and let them all run free for the day.

While Jane was living in Africa, she never stopped wanting to work with living animals in the wild. Since she and the Leakeys had returned from the Oldu-vai Gorge, Dr. Leakey had talked to her about a group of chimpanzees living near the shores of a lake in another country, Tanganyika. Dr. Leakey was very curious about how the chimps led their lives and asked Jane if she would like to observe the animals in their natural habitat. Since humans and chimpanzees are similar in many ways, Dr. Leakey hoped that learning more about the animals would reveal more information about human beings.

There were many obstacles to overcome, however, before Jane could begin her study of the chimpanzees. First, Dr. Leakey had to raise money to fund the project; then, Jane had to return to school in England to learn as much about chimps as possible. The government of Tanganyika also had to agree to the project and give Jane permission to study the animals.

After an adventurous and exciting year in Africa, Jane returned to England to begin her studies and await word from Dr. Leakey.

STILL MORE WAITING

Jane spent several months in England, learning about chimpanzees and observing them at the London Zoo. She spent hours watching the animals, noting how they behaved in captivity. She became concerned about how chimps were treated in zoos and what their lives were like in cages. She told herself that one day she would work to improve the lives of chimps in zoos. She felt that no animals should be forced to live in cramped, confined spaces.

Jane read a lot about chimps during her stay in England, but almost everything she studied was about the primates in captivity, not in the wild. She found only one person who had observed chimps in their natural setting, but he only watched for two months and did not learn very much. Jane claimed that, "the more I read [about chimpanzees] the more I realized how intelligent chimpanzees really are. Everyone agreed that they are more like human beings than any other creature alive today." Jane felt incredibly lucky, for soon she would be studying the chimps in their own habitat in the forest.

She waited and waited until finally Dr. Leakey wrote to say that he had gathered enough money to fund the project. He had also secured permission from the

Jane Goodall realized early that cages were not proper homes for chimpanzees.

government in Tanganyika (by now called *Tanzania* after merging with Zanzibar) that Jane could study and observe in the Gombe Stream Game Reserve. Getting the government to agree had not been easy and Dr. Leakey was required to promise the officials that Jane would not work in the preserve by herself.

Jane had to choose a companion to live and work with her in Africa. She chose her mother, who had visited Jane the year she spent in Kenya and was anxious to return to the continent. Vanne agreed to stay a few months with Jane, enough time, she hoped, to see her daughter established in her new position. Mother and daughter packed their things and flew to Nairobi where Dr. Leakey was waiting for them.

Once there, they had to make a few arrangements, including buying and packing supplies. Jane purchased several notebooks in which she could record her observations. She also had to buy green and brown clothes that would blend into the colors of the forest.

Jane and Vanne were set to go when they received some very disappointing news. Dr. Leakey told them he had gotten a telegram from Tanganyika saying that fishermen were fighting over fishing rights on the lake, the same lake where the two women would set up camp. While the scientist tried to smooth out the problems, he sent Jane and Vanne to observe vervet monkeys on an abandoned island in the middle of Lake Victoria in Kenya. About a month passed before Jane received word from Dr. Leakey that she could finally go to Gombe and begin studying the chimpanzees.

The journey to Gombe took several days, but finally Jane, Vanne, and a botanist from the museum in Kenya, Bernard Verdcout, arrived in Kigoma, a town close to the Reserve. After settling into a small hotel, the party discovered that government officials had once again postponed their trip to Gombe.

There had been a rebellion in the Belgian Congo (now Zaire) and it was not safe to travel through there as the rebels were killing many people. Jane, her mother, and Bernard stayed at the hotel until the authorities decided it was safe for them to travel to Gombe.

Bernard helped the two women stow all their gear in the boat that would carry them along the shores of Lake Tanganyika to their camp. Jane stated at that point, "Finally we were on the last stage of the long journey from England, via Lake Victoria, to Chimpanzee Land!"

AFRICA:
THE HEART OF DISCOVERY

BEGINNING A LIFE WITH THE CHIMPANZEES OF GOMBE

July 16, 1960, was a very important day in the life of twenty-six-year-old Jane Goodall. It was the first time she set foot on the sandy beach along the shore of Lake Tanganyika in the Gombe National Park. Her life with the chimpanzees was about to begin.

Helped by two Tanzanians who worked in the park, Jane and her mother found a suitable spot to set up their tent. Before they had left Kigoma, they had hired a cook, Dominic, who would prepare their meals and help them if any problems arose with local fisherman. After they set up camp, Jane set off for her first walk through the forest and hills that would become so familiar to her over the next thirty-five years. A fire had recently burned away much of the vegetation, so walking through the forest was quite easy.

On her first trek, Jane encountered a troop of baboons, barking *waa-hoo* when they saw her, and a red-gold bushbuck,

Jane lends a hand with camp chores in Gombe Stream National Park, Tanzania

which is a small forest antelope. She did not see any chimpanzees, but looked long and hard from a high ridge at the forest down below where she planned to explore for the animals the next day.

Back at camp, Jane and Vanne ate their dinner around the campfire before settling in for a restful night's sleep in their tent. The day had been full of new experiences and possibilities and they were very tired.

The next day, with a Tanzanian companion name Adolf by her side, Jane spotted two chimps feeding in a tree. Frightened by the strangers, the two animals fled as soon as they caught sight of the humans. For several days after that Jane saw no chimps. She was convinced that when they became aware of her presence, they disappeared into the

Jane keeps a scrapbook of life with the chimps at Gombe.

dense forest. It would take many months before the chimps were comfortable in her presence.

Jane went to the forest every day for several months, but the chimps ran away. Finally, Jane convinced a local game ranger that she needed to explore the forest alone. She told him the chimps would be more comfortable with one person than two and that she needed to establish a relationship with the chimps in her own way. The game ranger agreed.

Every morning after a small breakfast, Jane set off in search of the chimps. She spent much of her time at a place called the Peak, where she had the best view of the forest. She could see the chimps moving through the trees and could hear their calls to one another.

By watching from her post, she learned many things about how the animals lived. She discovered that they moved about in small groups of no more than about six chimps. The groups usually consisted of a mother with her children and two or three males. Sometimes, groups came together to feed at a tree laden with sweet fruit. When the groups joined they became very excited and made a lot of noise. Jane had no problem locating them in such large packs.

Jane soon realized that the groups she watched from the Peak were part of a larger group, called a community. There were about fifty chimps in the community she had found. After a day of frenzied feeding, when the chimps had built nests for themselves in the trees,

Members of a chimpanzee family group are very closely bonded.

One of the Gombe chimps enjoys a tasty snack.

Jane would climb down to the feeding spot and collect samples of the leaves, fruit and flowers they had eaten. Jane discovered that chimpanzees eat all kinds of plants, including seeds, stems, and blossoms, but that they also eat insects and occasionally meat. Before her research, scientists thought chimps ate only plants.

THE CHIMPANZEES HAVE NOTHING TO FEAR
After months of quiet observation, the chimps slowly began to realize that Jane was not a creature to fear; but even though they became comfortable with Jane in their presence, it was a full year before they would let her come within several hundred feet of them. In that time, Jane discovered that all kinds of other animals shared the forest with the

chimps, including monkeys, squirrels, mongooses, porcupines, snakes, rats, and mice.

The Peak began to feel like home to Jane and she spent many nights sleeping up there so she could awake with the chimpanzees at dawn. When the chimps began bending branches in the trees at night to make their sleeping nests, Jane pulled a blanket out of her tin trunk and herself fell asleep to the sounds of the night forest.

After her mother returned to England, Jane had no time to be lonely because there was so much work to do. One night, on retiring to camp, Jane was told by Dominic that a big male chimp had walked over to her tent and taken the bunch of bananas that Dominic had put out for her dinner. It was the first time a chimp had visited the camp. The next day, Jane stayed in camp to see if the chimp would return for more. Sure enough, around four o'clock in the afternoon, the banana thief appeared again.

The chimp was very familiar to Jane. He was a male chimp with a white beard that she had named David Greybeard. He ate palm nuts in a nearby tree for a little while then took the bananas Jane put out for him. In about a month, David actually took a banana from Jane's hand. From that point on, getting close to the chimps became easier for Jane. Other chimps were curious and, of course, hungry for free bananas. Soon they allowed Jane to get closer to them.

Once Jane could get closer to the chimps, she could carefully study how they behaved both in groups and alone.

David Greybeard makes a daring raid into Jane's camp in search of bananas.

She noted how at many times during the day chimps loved to play, as the female she'd named Flo did with her children, and how others led a more solitary life, on the fringes of the group. Often high-ranking male chimps had to fight to maintain their power over the group and were very brutal toward their fellow primates. For the most part, a chimp's daily life could be compared to a human's. They woke in the morning and ate breakfast, then groomed and cleaned each other. After that, they searched for and gathered more food, took naps, played into the afternoon, communicated by making sounds, and looked for a comfortable place to sleep at night.

One day, as Jane was following David Greybeard, she made one of her most exciting discoveries. She saw David using a blade of grass to pull termites out of a mound. He poked the blade into the mound, pulled it out as the insects clung to the grass with their jaws, and then he ate the juicy bugs. When the grass became too droopy, he used a stick instead. He made a tool to get food, something that scientists believed only humans could do.

While Jane had many peaceful days tracking through the forest after the chimps, there were times when they became fearful of her presence. She was always careful to appear non-threatening to the animals, but a chimpanzee, like any other animal, could act unpredictably. Over time, Jane had been beaten, hit, kicked, and charged at by the chimps, but fortunately was never seriously hurt. It is important to remember

Rolling around and playing games is a very important part of a chimp's day.

Termites make a tasty snack and these chimps know just how to "fish" for them using a blade of grass.

that a full-grown male chimpanzee, while standing no more than four feet tall, is three times as strong as a grown man.

Jane had many adventures in the forest in her early years at Gombe. Each night after dinner, she would record the day's observations in notebooks while the information was still fresh in her mind. Keeping notes in her journal was a very important part of her research on chimps.

As time passed, Jane began to recognize each chimp and gave them names. Some of her early friends included David Greybeard, William, Goliath, and old Flo, one of the most well-respected females in the community. While Flo was not beautiful, with her puffy nose and ragged ears, she had many children who were prominent members of her group including daughter Fifi, and sons Figan and Faben. From Flo, Jane learned that female chimpanzees have a baby only once every five or six years, and that they have more than one mate.

VISITORS ARRIVE

The chimps were making regular visits to camp when Dr. Louis Leakey told Jane that the National Geographic Society in America, which was helping to fund the project was sending someone to film her and the chimps at Gombe. Jane's work was beginning to draw attention from around the world and people wanted to know more about her life with the chimpanzees.

The man who made the film about Gombe was a baron from Holland

After a long day in the field, Jane records her observations by flashlight.

*Capturing scenes of daily Gombe life, filmmaker
Hugo van Lawick directs his camera toward a curious baboon.*

named Hugo van Lawick. He and Jane spent a lot of time together while he shot the film and the two eventually fell in love. A year later, in 1966, after Jane had returned to England to finish her studies, she and Hugo were married.

After Jane received her degree in animal behavior, she and Hugo returned to Gombe and the chimpanzees. When she got back, Jane was very excited to see that Flo had given birth to a son, Flint. In addition to being very happy for Flo, Jane knew it was a perfect opportunity to study the child-rearing methods of chimpanzees. Flint clung to Flo's stomach when he was a tiny baby, but when he got a little older, his older sister, Fifi, was allowed to hold and groom him. Fifi was learning how to be a good mother while taking care of her little brother.

Flo's four-year-old son Flint tries to crowd into a nest Flo has made for her and her new baby.

Bound by three generations of strong ties, Flo, Freud, Fifi, and Flint spend a quiet family moment together.

Jane's son, Hugo Eric Louis, better known as "Grub," spent his early years at Gombe before returning to England at age nine.

When Flint began to walk, at six months old, he started to play with his two older brothers, Figan and Faben. He also played with other chimps in the community, but if they were ever too rough, Flo was right there to protect him. Most female chimps are very attentive and kind mothers, but some females are not so loving. For example, a chimpanzee named Passion was a neglectful and distant mother and, as a result, her daughter, Pom, was sulky and needy.

In 1967, after observing the maternal behavior of the chimps, Jane herself became a mother. Her son, who was born Hugo Eric Louis, was called Grub by everyone in the camp. Jane was very careful when Grub was a baby and lived in Gombe, as chimps have been known to eat babies. As far as a chimp is concerned there is no difference between a baby baboon and a human baby. Despite the risks, Grub had a wonderful childhood along the shores of Lake Tanganyika.

Jane's work with the chimpanzees was so well known by the beginning of the 1970s, that students of animal behavior from all over the world wanted to join her in Gombe. She was happy to accommodate them for short periods of time as she needed help with the enormous amount of work that studying the chimpanzees entailed. There were records to keep, different groups to observe, and a large number of observations to write up. Jane found the students who worked with her at Gombe to be dedicated and passionate about chimpanzees.

After years of careful observation, Jane is able to share intimate moments with once wary chimps.

Grooming and cleaning is an important part of the chimps' daily routine.

TROUBLE AT GOMBE

For several years life at Gombe was peaceful and productive. Thanks to the help of the foreign students and several dedicated Africans, Jane was able to spend a lot of time with Grub. Unfortunately, in 1974, she and Hugo separated and divorced, but remained good friends. Her work kept her in Africa, while his required him to travel all over the world.

Jane soon remarried, an Englishman named Derek Bryceson, who had lost the use of his legs during World War II when his plane was shot down. Derek had a house in Dar es Salaam, the capital of Tanzania, where Jane still spends much of her time today. Derek was the director of Tanzania National Park and much loved and respected by almost all who met him. Tragically, he died of cancer only a few years after they were married.

The years between 1974 and 1977 were perhaps the bleakest years in Gombe's history. Not only were a good portion of the chimps that Jane had studied since the 1960s killed by attacks from other communities, but she had also witnessed the gruesome murders of several chimpanzee babies by cannibalistic Passion and Pom. About this time Jane said, "The intercommunity violence and cannibalism that took place at Gombe . . . for ever [changed] my view of chimpanzee nature. For so many years I had believed that chimpanzees, while showing uncanny similarities to humans in many ways, were, by and large, rather 'nicer' than us."

In addition, during 1975, rebels from across Lake Tanganyika in Zaire landed on the beach at Gombe and kidnapped seven students. The students were eventually released, but it was a very tense time for Jane, the students, and the field staff. Studying the chimps was very difficult as Jane had to spend much of her time in Dar es Salaam for safety.

When events finally calmed down, Jane had to rethink how to continue her research at Gombe. She sent Grub to live with his grandmother in England when he was nine so he could go to school there. Jane spent every holiday with him, but they lived apart.

A BETTER LIFE FOR ANIMALS

WORKING TOWARD THE FUTURE

For the past fifteen years, Jane has continued her work, studying and recording the day-to-day events of chimpanzee life at Gombe, but she also spends a good part of her year traveling and lecturing about the animals. The center in the park has become firmly established, with students and journalists from all over the world spending time there, learning about the chimps. One of Jane's priorities now is to raise money so the work at Gombe can continue.

She has also become an advocate for chimpanzee rights in zoos and laboratory testing, just as she said she would in the late 1950s. Thanks to her efforts, the lives of chimps in both the United States and Europe are greatly improved. Jane has even started a group called ChimpanZoo, where students, zoo keepers, and volunteers study the behavior of chimpanzees just as she studies them in Gombe. Jane is also the founder of an

One of the researchers holds a young chimp.

institute that bears her name. The Jane Goodall Institute, based in the United States, raises money to help rescue and relocate chimpanzees in Africa. In addition, she has recently begun a program called Roots and Shoots for very young children to learn more about the natural world. The program has branches in more than twenty countries, and there are over 250 Roots and Shoots groups.

Jane's lecture tours are very hectic, but even if she did not need to raise money, she would still travel and share what she knows about the chimpanzees. When she is not traveling, Jane lives in her house in Dar es Salaam and at the research center at Gombe.

Jane's life is very busy and sometimes, as in the past, her life can be difficult and sad. "But," as she says, "all my

Through her animal rights program, Roots & Shoots, *Jane teaches children from Africa to America about how important it is to care for animals.*

problems fade away when I follow the chimps deep into the forest and sit with them. The birds sing. The wind whispers in the leaves. Little lizards move up and down the old trunks of trees. That, for me, is like a visit to heaven."

We have learned so much from Jane Goodall because of her lifelong love, dedication, and curiosity about animals. She has spent decades studying the lives of our closest living animal relatives, the chimpanzees. Thanks to her, we know much more about these magnificent animals and about ourselves.

To Learn More About Jane Goodall and Chimpanzees

About Jane Goodall

Birnbaum, Bette. *Jane Goodall and the Wild Chimpanzees*. Chatham, New Jersey: Raintree Steck-Vaughn, 1989.

Fromer, Julie. *Jane Goodall: Living With the Chimps*. New York: TFC Books, 1992.

Fuchs, Carol. *Jane Goodall: The Chimpanzee's Friend*. Vero Beach, Florida: Rourke, 1993.

Goodall, Jane. *My Life With Chimpanzees*. New York: Minstrel Books, 1988.

About Chimpanzees

McCormick, Maxine. *Chimpanzees*. New York: Crestwood, 1990.

Petty, Kate. *Chimpanzees*. New York: Franklin Watts, 1990.

Stone, Lynn. *Chimpanzees*. Vero Beach, Florida: Rourke, 1990.

Index

Page numbers for illustrations are in boldface

ABOUT THE AUTHOR

Elizabeth Ferber's work has appeared in *The New York Times Book Review, The Washington Post, New York Magazine,* and other national publications. She is the author of several books including biographies of Yasir Arafat and Steven Spielberg, and the novel *Soon Found, Soon Lost.* She is a co-author of *The Walker's Companion,* a Nature Company field guide. She lives in Brooklyn, New York.